Th

Gingerbread
Nativity

Barnabas for Children® is a registered word mark and the logo is a registered device mark of
The Bible Reading Fellowship.
Text copyright © Renita Boyle 2013
Illustrations by Christine Reissland, © BRF 2013
Cover photographs copyright © 2013: front (angel) © Kim Ayres, others © Renita Boyle;
back © Kim Ayres.

The author asserts the moral right
to be identified as the author of this work

Published by
The Bible Reading Fellowship
15 The Chambers, Vineyard
Abingdon OX14 3FE
United Kingdom
Tel: +44 (0)1865 319700
Email: enquiries@brf.org.uk
Website: www.brf.org.uk
BRF is a Registered Charity

ISBN 978 0 85746 161 2

First published 2013
10 9 8 7 6 5 4 3 2 1 0

Acknowledgments
Unless otherwise stated, scripture quotations are taken from the Contemporary English
Version of the Bible published by HarperCollins Publishers, copyright © 1991, 1992, 1995
American Bible Society.

The paper used in the production of this publication was supplied by mills that source their
raw materials from sustainably managed forests. Soy-based inks were used in its printing and
the laminate film is biodegradable.

A catalogue record for this book is available from the British Library

Printed in Singapore by Craft Print International Ltd

The Gingerbread Nativity

A four-week exploration of Advent

Renita Boyle

For Helen.
Thank you for your friendship, tea and the
perfect gingerbread recipe!

Acknowledgments

Any project is only as wonderful as those who make it happen. My particular thanks to my beloved, Eric, who kept calm throughout the chaos that engulfed our kitchen, and to my son, Jude, who proved to be an amazing baker. I am also deeply thankful for the families who helped me to develop and pilot this resource: Hazel Cannon, Lorna and Lindsay; Willa Cannon, Kirsty and Andrew; Lisa Dunn and Rory; Helen Ferguson, Heather and Sandy; Lisa Martin, Erin and Bob; June Robinson, Emma and Kathryn; Jude, Marti, Bryony and Keira.

I would also like to thank portrait photographer, Kim Ayres (http://kimayres.co.uk), for the delightful images he has produced of our completed projects. You can see more of these images (and others that we took ourselves) at www.renitaboyle.com and www. facebook.com/RenitaBoyleBibleTalesAndTunes.

A web search for 'gingerbread nativity scenes' proved inspiring and provided a mass of information and generational wisdom. While it would be difficult to credit a single source, I would particularly like to recommend the following:

- www.gingerbread-house-heaven.com
- *Biscuiteers Book of Iced Biscuits* by Harriet Hastings and Sarah Moore (Kyle Cathie, 2010)
- *Decorated Cookies (Twenty to Make)* by Lisa Slatter (Search Press, 2010)

★

Contents

Foreword

This book has all the right ingredients—recipes, techniques, stories, suggestions, templates—but one thing is missing: the wonderful, comforting, nostalgic aroma of freshly baked spicy gingerbread. Bring on the scratch and sniff page! More seriously, I recommend this book to children's and family workers, all-age ministry leaders, Messy Church teams, individuals and the whole family, because we all have a challenge.

Having recently visited Germany, I particularly recall the beautiful bakery shop windows. We salivated at the displays of creative cakes with handwritten descriptions, and when we entered the shop itself there was even more to tempt us.

I feel that the challenge as a Christian at Christmas is a huge one. We know that more and more people of all ages celebrate Christmas but are unaware of its true meaning. Who is going to tell them? It is our individual duty to do so. Jesus asks each of us to share his story.

This book is a great tool to use in this way. Imagine this book to be the bakery shop window. Who will you invite to look in with you? Who needs to know what else is inside?

The birth of Jesus is so important, and yet can we assume that all ages are looking in the window of discovery? Unfortunately they are not. They are just walking on by. We need to lead them and start them on this journey of discovery.

The world is full of instant gratification. Today's technology allows us to view, hear, purchase, share and much more, just with the click of a mouse. Yet at the same time we are finding that there is a resurgence in creating homemade gifts, craft making, baking, knitting and sewing. All ages are discovering the pleasure and reward of making something rather than buying it off the shelf.

New websites, blogs, TV programmes, knit and natter groups and workshops are popping up, inviting you to have a go, learn together, and create something for yourself or friends and family. Indeed, one of the core values of Messy Church is creativity, and all ages are responding to the invitation and coming back for more.

I encourage you to trust in God and get stuck in. Trust in Renita, a renowned storyteller and practitioner in all things creative. Trust in this book and do what it says on the tin!

Jane Leadbetter is the author of Messy Nativity *(BRF, 2012) and runs L19: Messy Church and L19: Who Let The Dads Out?*

Introduction

Advent is a time of spiritual reflection and preparation, a time to savour the promise of Christmas Day. Gingerbread houses and figures can be fun to make and sweet to eat. Mix these together and you have the perfect recipe for a memorable and tasty exploration of Advent. The possibilities are endless and the process is engaging for all involved.

The Gingerbread Nativity is ideal for Sunday schools and midweek clubs. The resource offers a four-session exploration of Advent through the building and decorating of a gingerbread nativity scene or scenes (depending on how many your group choose to make). The scene includes a stable with figures of Mary, Joseph, an ox, angels, a donkey, stars, shepherds, sheep and the baby Jesus. Figures of a camel and wise men can be added if you wish.

Section 1 offers instructions, recipes and top tips for mixing, rolling, cutting, baking, building and decorating gingerbread. It also includes guidance on how to make a 'fake' out of cardboard as an example to work from or as an alternative to working with gingerbread.

Section 2 includes Advent reflections and discussion starters for each of the four weekly sessions. There is also a fifth session, which may be used as the basis for a gingerbread-themed family service.

Whether you choose to use the material in four weekly sessions, as a half-day workshop or in a Messy Church environment, with a small group or large, single-age or all-age, at home or as part of a community event, *The Gingerbread Nativity* is sure to inspire tasty Advent fun for everyone.

★ **Section 1** ★

The project

Before you start

Making gingerbread projects from scratch is fun, but planning and preparation are vital for a successful outcome. This resource includes templates for a gingerbread stable and 13 other pieces. A larger version of the stable and figures can be made by using the templates available to download from www.barnabasinchurches. org.uk/9780857461612/.

The gingerbread process itself involves two main stages:

- Making and baking the nativity shapes.
- Building and decorating the nativity scene.

This resource assumes that most, if not all, of the making and baking stage will be done for your group before Advent, and the building and decorating stage will be done by your group during Advent. Families may choose to make and bake their own gingerbread pieces or you may want to enlist a few parents or a team of experienced bakers to mix the dough and make and bake the shapes for your group. Members of the Women's Institute, scouts, guides, youth club or even a team from the community may be happy to take up the challenge of preparing and baking the dough.

If you choose to involve your group in the making and baking stage, you will need to think about how best to achieve this in your own circumstances. You may, for example, want to host a special workshop day for your group in the autumn and freeze the pieces until Advent. Children will enjoy the added anticipation in the run-up to Christmas and the sense of achievement in being involved throughout the whole process. Alternatively, you may simply wish to add a few shorter baking sessions to your programme for the creation of special pieces, such as stained-glass-effect stars or angel wings. Simply ask your baking team to mix the required amount of dough and freeze it until you are ready to use it with your group.

Before you commit to any part of the project, you will want to consider the size, age range and abilities of your group; identify the resources you have and those you will need to find. Also, you will need to consider how you will overcome possible time and space constraints and any health and safety issues that may arise. It is vital that you read 'Health, hygiene and safety' (see page 14) for crucial guidance on safeguarding as well as the edibility of the end product.

You will need to decide how many nativity scenes your group will create (one per child, per pair or per family or one for the whole group), as well as the number of characters you want to include. You may limit your scene to Mary, Joseph, baby Jesus, a donkey, a sheep and a star. Conversely, if you feel you need more pieces, you can make as many sheep, stars or angels as you like. These may not be included in the scene itself but could be used to decorate a Christmas tree or, if the gingerbread is fresh, served up to eat during a gingerbread family service. The choice is yours.

The templates included will work best if they are traced on to and cut from clear acetate. To adapt the size of the pieces in your project, simply reduce or increase the size of the templates. You may, for example, wish to create a smaller (or even mini) nativity scene, or a giant slotted star.

Cutters may also be used, at least in part. A web search for 'nativity cookie cutters' will bring up a variety of products and information on how to purchase them. Stars and angels are easily obtained. The templates in this resource have been designed to accompany the teaching material. Should you wish to use a set of nativity cutters instead, you will need to ensure that it includes all the shapes required.

The timescale and scope of the making and baking stage will depend largely on what you choose to do.

The building and decorating stage should be achievable in four one-hour sessions. However, the project is progressive. If your group does not complete all the pieces in a given session, you can simply continue to work on them in the next. For example, the stable may be constructed in a single session but may also need time to set before decoration. Indeed, depending on your group, it may be a good idea to plan an extra 'finishing off' session towards the end for completing bits and pieces.

Dividing your group into teams of two or three will work well, both for individual tasks (decorating individual shapes) and in cooperative tasks where more hands make light work (building the stable).

Session plans

Four main teaching sessions are outlined in Section 2 of this book. Each session focuses on a portion of the nativity story and includes a themed reflection and suggestions for discussion as you build and decorate your nativity scene(s) together. You need not aim to cover everything in the plan; draw from it whatever will encourage a spiritually meaningful discussion as you work. For example, younger groups may simply enjoy hearing the story and chatting about it, while older groups may enjoy exploring the theme in more depth.

NB: You may choose to read the story from the Bible passage given, use a child-friendly Bible storybook or simply tell the story in your own words. References are included for *The Barnabas Children's Bible* (Barnabas for Children, 2012), which is both clear and concise.

Family service

The family service is an opportunity for your group to display their gingerbread nativities and share the joy of the Christmas story with the church, community and other invited family and friends. Ideas are included for decorating the church or other gathering-space, involving your group in presenting the nativity story (complete with a gingerbread nativity scene and hymns or songs) and giving a family-friendly children's talk based on the story of the wise men's visit.

★

Health, hygiene and safety

It is the responsibility of those working with children and vulnerable adults to keep them safe. Please ensure that the child protection and safeguarding policies and procedures specified by your organisation are known and followed.

This teaching resource covers the month of Advent, and the decoration stage is progressive over four or five weekly sessions. Therefore, for health and hygiene reasons, the finished nativity scene itself is intended for display purposes only and not to be eaten. In any case, the gingerbread recipe used without a raising agent (such as baking powder) helps the pieces to keep their shape while baking but results in a texture that is quite tough to eat.

Extra and delightfully edible pieces (particularly stars, sheep and angels) can, however, be baked with the proper raising agent and stored and decorated for consumption within the specified guidelines. As a general rule, raw gingerbread dough will stay fresh in a fridge for approximately three days; it can also be stored in a freezer for three months, ready for baking at a later stage. Baked gingerbread will stay fresh in an airtight container for approximately one month; it can also be frozen for up to three months, ready for defrosting, constructing and decorating at a later stage. This is particularly important to know if you intend to serve at least some of your baked gingerbread creations as part of a gingerbread family service, in Messy Church or during other community gatherings.

Attention to dietary concerns, food hygiene and environmental safety is vital during this project. It is especially important to identify whether anyone in your group has a food allergy, is sensitive to food colourings or has diabetes or other dietary restrictions.

It will be tempting for your group to nibble while they work.

Use tasting spoons rather than fingers, and offer healthy snacking options as an alternative.

If food allergies or restrictions prove problematic, you may want to adapt the recipes included (see pages 31–36), find suitable alternative recipes of your own and/or choose decorating materials with greater care. If you would rather not work with food at all, you can simply use the templates in this resource to make a fake nativity scene out of cardboard (see page 16) and skip the 'Taste of the day' at the end of each session.

Health and safety summary

- All policies and procedures for safeguarding and child protection should be followed.
- Food preparation environments should be carefully chosen and food hygiene certificates should be in place. Children should be supervised by the appropriate number of adults for the size of the group at all times.
- Clear instructions should be given throughout.
- Tasks should be assigned and taken in turn to avoid confusion and arguments.
- Children should be kept a safe distance away from hot ovens and pans, and great care should be taken when using potentially dangerous equipment.
- Hands should be thoroughly washed before handling foodstuffs and rewashed by anyone who leaves the room or touches their nose, mouth and so on.
- Loose-fitting clothing should be avoided; aprons and closed-toe shoes should be worn.
- Hair should be pulled back off the face.
- Work spaces and tools should be tidied as you go along.
- Food should be stored safely at the end of each session.

★

Making and baking the gingerbread

Make a trial-run model

Making and decorating a cardboard model before embarking on the gingerbread project can be very helpful. It will give you a good idea of how the nativity scene fits together and it will give your group inspiration for decorating their own. It is also a good alternative if you feel that a full-on gingerbread project is too difficult for your group to undertake. To make a model out of cardboard, refer to the templates on pages 75–87 and adapt in the following ways.

* Make a base for your project. A piece of wood covered with foil, a foam board or a baking tray work well. The base will need to be big enough to accommodate the whole project, including stable, people and animals. It will make decorating and moving your project much easier.
* Use thick corrugated cardboard for your pieces.
* Trace the templates provided on to clear plastic acetate and cut them out.
* Use your plastic templates to trace and cut the pieces you need from cardboard.
* Remember to cut out windows, doors or other features.
* Tape or hot-glue the structure of the stable together; stick together any other pieces as required. Many mistakes you might otherwise have made with the gingerbread can be easily spotted and corrected at this stage.
* Decorate with paper, fabric, marking pens and other collage materials.

- Keep the model as a visual aid for your real gingerbread nativity.
- If you will not be using cutters, copy and cut another set of templates, ready to use with the gingerbread.

Mixing the dough

Refer to the gingerbread recipe given on page 31 or use a recipe of your own. Decide how many nativity sets you want to make and work out the quantity of dough you will need. A rough quantity guide is given, although it will vary according to how many pieces you choose to make and what size you choose to make them.

Gingerbread dough can be mixed by hand or with a food processer with a paddle attachment. In either case, ensure that you have read the recipe before you start and have the necessary equipment (see list on page 30) and the ingredients to hand. Mix the dough as instructed in the recipe.

Storing the dough for use later

Gingerbread dough is most pliable on the day that it is made. However, it can also be stored for up to three days in the fridge or up to three months in the freezer before use.

To store the dough in a refrigerator or freezer *before* rolling it out, divide it into even portions and pat each one into a squarish shape. This will make the dough easier to roll out when the time comes. Then, double-wrap each portion in clingfilm or place into a zip-top bag, date it and refrigerate or freeze. When you are ready to roll the dough, simply remove it from the fridge or freezer and allow it to sit at room temperature until it is pliable.

To store the dough in a refrigerator or freezer *after* it has been rolled out, divide it into even portions and roll each one on top of a sheet of parchment paper as described below. Then move the rolled dough (complete with parchment) to a baking tray, double-wrap and refrigerate or freeze. You will need to make space in your fridge or freezer for the tray to lie flat. Several layers of dough can be stacked on top of each other with parchment in between.

When you are ready to cut the dough, simply remove it from the fridge or freezer and allow it to sit at room temperature until it is pliable.

Chilling the dough for same-day use

Gingerbread dough is usually chilled before rolling, because chilled dough is less sticky and easier to work with. Divide the dough into even portions and pat each into a squarish shape. Then wrap each portion in clingfilm or place into a zip-top bag and pop it into the fridge for between 20 minutes and two hours. When you are ready, remove the dough from the fridge and allow it to sit at room temperature until it is just pliable enough to roll.

Rolling the dough

To roll the dough, cut a sheet of baking parchment approximately the same size as the baking tray you will be using. Choose a flat rolling surface and a heavy rolling-pin. Place the parchment on top of the rolling surface and the dough on top of the parchment. Roll the dough with the rolling-pin. Sprinkle flour as necessary to reduce sticking. Rolling (and cutting) the dough on parchment will result in the easy transfer of a whole sheet of cut pieces to your baking tray. This method is particularly useful for large or delicate pieces that might otherwise tear or lose shape when transferred.

Roll the dough outward from the centre to form a rectangular shape of uniform thickness: 6mm (1/4 inch) for stable pieces and 3mm (1/8 inch) for other objects and characters. Try to cover the whole sheet of parchment with rolled dough. This will maximise the number of pieces you are able to cut and will minimise dough handling.

Chill or re-chill the rolled dough in a refrigerator until firm. This will ensure that shapes are easily cut and hold their shape while baking. Simply lift the parchment (complete with rolled dough) by opposite corners and place it on a baking tray. Then put the tray into the fridge. Several layers can be stored on top of each other with parchment in between.

Cutting the dough

Gather all of your templates (traced on to and cut from clear plastic acetate) and/or cutters before cutting the dough. Choose a safe cutting surface. Ensure that you are cutting the correct pieces from the correct type and thickness of dough, as outlined above: shapes for the stable should be at 6mm (1/4 inch) and all others at 3mm (1/8 inch). Remove a flattened sheet of dough from the fridge or freezer and allow it to soften just enough to cut.

You will be cutting your dough on top of the piece of parchment on which it has been rolled. Take some time to plan how you will lay your templates or cutters on the rolled dough before you begin. This will maximise the number of shapes you are able to cut and minimise waste. It is a good idea to keep 25mm (1 inch) between shapes for easier baking.

To prevent sticking, lightly dip cutters and templates in flour before cutting the dough. Use a straight-edged pizza cutter to cut out large straight-edged shapes, a smooth-bladed knife to cut around curvier shapes, or cutters that are pressed directly into the dough. Remember to cut out any windows or shapes within shapes, which you may want to leave empty or fill with crushed sweets for a stained-glass effect (see page 21).

Remove the surplus dough by lifting it carefully away from the parchment and place it in a plastic bag for re-rolling. If you have all the primary shapes you require, excess dough can be re-rolled, cut and baked into decorative shapes. For example, letters saying 'Jesus is born' can be attached to the roof of the stable.

Baking the dough

Choose edgeless baking trays for best results and ensure that trays are cooled between batches.

Lift your parchment (complete with cut shapes) by opposite corners and transfer it to a baking tray. This will ensure that there is no distortion or tearing of the dough. Bake as instructed in your chosen recipe.

Baked shapes should be slightly brown around the edges. After baking, transfer the parchment, with shapes, to a wire rack. Don't remove the shapes until they are completely cool.

Repeat the process until all the shapes you need are baked.

If a piece loses its shape too much while baking, you can attempt to rectify it. Place the template carefully on top of the shape while it is still warm and cut round it again.

The following directions apply for special shapes.

Dimensional shapes

The stable is constructed of several different shapes stuck together with mortar icing (a variation of royal icing). Other pieces are also made of two or more shapes. For example, donkey B is self-standing and is made from a gingerbread back, front and head, plus three round shop-bought biscuits (see page 80). These individual shapes are baked and stuck together with mortar icing.

Alternatively, you may choose to lay one dough shape on top of another (for example, a small star on top of a larger star) and bake them together. This will, of course, make shapes a bit thicker and increase baking time a little. However, it can produce a nice effect.

Glittered shapes

To produce baked shapes with a glittery or speckled effect, simply use your fingers to press edible glitter or hundreds-and-thousands into the shaped dough before baking. The stable walls, angel wings or dove can all be given extra flair in this way.

Stained-glass shapes

Some shapes are ideal for incorporating a stained-glass effect—for example, stars (page 82), angel wings (page 77) or crowns (page 86). Simply cut out a smaller shape within the whole shape, leaving a good edge all round the hole. Then take a variety of colourful boiled sweets and place them in a double-layer zip-top bag. Crush the sweets into powdered shards with a mallet. Pour the crushed sweets into the gap, level with the dough and touching the edges. The sweets will melt during baking and fill the gap, giving a stained-glass window effect.

Hanging shapes

Most shapes, particularly stars, can be easily adapted to hang on a tree. Poke a hole in the soft dough with the end of a straw and bake. Make sure that the hole is not too close to the edge and, while the dough is still warm, check that the hole has not closed in. If it has, simply push the straw through again. String a ribbon through the hole once the piece has hardened.

You can also hang a shape within a shape, such as a smaller star within a larger star. Ensure that both shapes are baked with a hole in them and attach the two shapes together with a ribbon.

Stacked shapes

Several sizes of the same shape can be stacked on top of one another to create objects. For example, several stacked stars can look like a tree. Bake several stars of different sizes and, with the biggest star at the bottom, ice them together.

Textured shapes

Interesting textures can be imprinted into the dough before baking. Place a textured item, such as string, lace or a doily, on top of the dough, roll it into the surface with a rolling pin and carefully remove to reveal the imprinted pattern.

Slotted shapes

Slotted biscuits slot together to make three-dimensional shapes or figures that can stand up on their own. For example, cut two star shapes from rolled dough and cut a slot into one or both of them. Once baked, slot the two together to form a three-dimensional star (see page 82).

Stand-up shapes

The simplest way to make a single-layer shape stand up is to mortar it to a wedge-shaped piece of gingerbread. Several of the pieces in this resource stand up in this way (see templates in the Appendix). Other self-standing shapes can be made by layering or 'sandwiching' two or more shaped biscuits together with mortar icing and decorating both outer sides. It can also work well to 'sandwich' a round or rectangular ready-made biscuit between two identical shapes (see page 80).

Storing baked shapes

It is a good idea to let baked shapes sit for a day before they are decorated. Indeed, as the baking for this project will be done in advance, you will want to think carefully about how to store the baked shapes until you are ready to use them with your group. The key to preserving baked gingerbread shapes successfully is to protect them from moisture and odours.

When the shapes are completely cool, layer them between baking parchment (up to three layers) and place them in an airtight plastic container. You can also store baked shapes in zip-top bags or double-wrap them in clingfilm. Baked gingerbread can be kept in a cool, dry place for up to a month or frozen for three months.

You will need to pack the shapes together in 'kits' in preparation for assembly. For example, all the shapes for the stable should be packed together as Kit 1 and labelled for easy identification; similarly, pack together all the shapes for the ox, including stands, as Kit 2, and so on. There will be 13 kits in total: details of all the pieces needed are given in the next chapter ('Building the nativity figures', pages 25–26). Packing shapes into kits is particularly useful if you are making several nativity scenes.

Allow frozen shapes to thaw in their containers or zip-top bags at room temperature. If they have become too soggy, re-crisp them in the oven for a few minutes and let them cool before assembly and decoration.

NB: Please ensure that gingerbread intended for consumption is prepared and stored properly and eaten within the specified time (see 'Health, hygiene and safety', page 14).

★

Building and decorating the nativity

The following instructions for building and decorating your nativity scene assume that your group will do this over four or five weekly sessions as directed. If you would rather build and decorate in a single half-day workshop or Messy Church environment, see 'Adapting for Messy Church' on pages 39–41.

Building the stable

Ensure that everyone has washed their hands and is adhering to the health, hygiene and safety principles (see page 14). Divide your group into teams of two or three and ensure that each team has plenty of workspace and a base for their project—a piece of wood covered with foil, a foam board or a baking tray. The base will need to be big enough to accommodate the whole project, including stable, people and animals. It will make decorating and moving your project much easier.

Give each team a set of baked shapes for the stable (Kit 1) and an icing bag (or two) filled with mortar icing. A plastic sandwich bag with a very small bit of one corner snipped off works well as an inexpensive and easy-to-use icing bag for little hands. Kit 1 includes four pieces: roof, back wall and two side walls. Refer to the template on page 75 and the trial-run model (if you have made one) to identify how the pieces of the stable join together and in what order.

Although almost any kind of icing can be used to decorate

gingerbread structures and shapes, mortar icing, a variation of royal icing (see page 32), is ideal for construction. It is soft enough to pipe and hardens with time. Mortar icing can be used to hold the walls and roof of the stable together, stick individual shapes together and stick decorative sweets to the gingerbread shapes. Mortar icing dries out easily, so it should be kept covered when not in use. Care should also be taken not to overwhip the icing or it will crack and crumble as it dries.

The basic principle is to pipe a thick (but not dripping) line of mortar icing to the edge of one of the two shapes that are to be joined together. Then the un-iced shape is pressed to the iced shape and held until the icing is partially set. This process is repeated until the stable walls are complete. The seams between shapes should also be well iced and the walls well set before the roof is added. It can be helpful to allow the icing to set along the edge for a while before assembly. To provide additional stability, you can also mortar the bottom edges of the walls to the base as you go along. It is also helpful to use food tins to prop the walls up until they are set firmly enough to stand on their own.

Building the nativity figures

Most of the figures are made of two or more shapes iced together. Give every team the kits of shapes that they need in each session. Refer to the templates on pages 76–87 and the model (if you have made one) to determine where to join the shapes. Stands are mortared to the figures with a thick line of icing at the join. Other shapes are mortared together by piping a thick blob of icing to one shape and gently pressing another shape on top. It is a good idea to lay the main shape flat and decorate it before icing it to a stand or another shape.

The complete list of gingerbread figures needed is as follows.

- Session 1: Ox (see Kit 2 templates on page 76).
- Session 1: Angel A, B or C (see Kit 3 templates on page 77).
- Session 1: Mary (see Kit 4 templates on page 78).
- Session 2: Joseph (see Kit 5 templates on page 79).
- Session 2: Donkey A or B (see Kit 6 templates on page 80).
- Session 3: Baby Jesus and manger (see Kit 7 templates on page 81).
- Session 3: Star A, B or C (see Kit 8 templates on page 82, or use a star-shaped biscuit cutter).
- Session 4: Shepherd (see Kit 9 templates on page 83).
- Session 4: Sheep (see Kit 10 templates on page 84).
- Family service: Camel (see Kit 11 templates on page 85).
- Family service: Wise men (see Kit 12 templates on page 86).
- Family service: Large or specially decorated star (see Kit 13 template on page 87).

Decorating the nativity

Although every scene will be decorated differently, planning and preparation are vital for a smooth and enjoyable experience. Before you begin to decorate, you will want to make sure that you have everything you need. Icing recipes are provided on pages 32–36 and possible ideas for decoration on pages 28–29. Deciding ahead of time which of these your group are likely to use will help you to gather, purchase and prepare what you need for each session. The list may also inspire a few ideas of your own.

Before you start, ensure that everyone has washed their hands and is adhering to the health, hygiene and safety principles (see page 14). Also ensure that you have the necessary equipment (see page 30), workspace and items with which to decorate. Sweets should be unwrapped and placed in separate bowls before you begin.

Using icing

Royal icing

Royal icing hardens when dry and is used, in differing thicknesses, both to build and to decorate. It is thinned with water, a few drops at a time, to achieve the consistency needed to mortar, pipe, flood or paint. It can also be tinted any colour using liquid food colouring or gels. Although royal icing can be made ahead of time, it is best used on the day that it is made to avoid separation. It dries out easily so it should be kept in an airtight container and covered when not in use.

Fondant icing

Fondant icing is a smooth, dough-like paste. It is rolled, cut into shapes and attached (with dabs of royal icing) rather than spread or piped like other icings. It can also be tinted any colour (see page 35) and draped to look like cloth (or a blanket of snow). Although fondant icing never completely hardens, it will keep its shape much like soft clay. It is ideal for clothing, hair, faces and just about any other decorative shape you can imagine.

Ready-to-roll fondant icing is available in an array of colours and may be purchased online, from speciality shops or the supermarket. Unused fondant icing may be kept for up to four weeks but must be double-wrapped tightly in clingfilm before being placed in a zip-lock bag (ensuring that all the air is squeezed out) and stored in a cool, dry place. Fondant icing should not be frozen.

Glacé icing

Glacé icing is simple to make and can be coloured and flavoured to suit. It remains quite soft so it should be used for projects that are designed to be eaten within a day or two of decoration. It is ideal for on-the-spot congregational involvement, such as icing a gingerbread star to eat at the end of a gingerbread family service.

Decorating ideas

Your gingerbread nativity scene may be decorated in any way you can imagine. However, this list will provide a helpful starting-point and may inspire a few ideas of your own.

- Icing: a variation of royal icing may be used to mortar, pipe, flood or paint; fondant may be used to drape or cover.
- Stable walls: breadsticks, square savoury crackers, rectangular biscuits
- Roof and stable floor: wheat-based breakfast cereals (flakes or shredded), rice cereals (thatch), chocolate squares (tiles), sprinkle stars
- Windows: crushed hard-boiled sweets or lollipops (see stained-glass window effect, page 21)
- Shutters: sticks of chewing gum, rectangular biscuits
- Fences and posts: chocolate finger sticks, breadsticks, toffee strips
- Logs: mini chocolate cake rolls, mini chocolate flake bars
- Snow or frost: icing sugar, edible glitter
- Angel wings: mini sweets or chocolate drops, edible glitter, hundreds and thousands (can be lightly pressed into the dough before baking or sprinkled on top after baking), crushed hard sweets or lollipops (stained-glass window effect)
- Star centres: edible glitter, crushed hard-boiled sweets or lollipops (stained-glass window effect)
- Shepherds' staff: mini sticks of coloured rock, chocolate matchsticks, breadsticks
- Water: microwave a hard sweet (blue or transparent) on baking parchment until melted, blue gummy or jelly sweets rolled flat, blue sprinkles on blue icing

- Straw: broken up or shredded wheat-based cereals
- Animal hooves: small round chocolates (cut in half), round pastille or mint sweets
- Animal poo: small bean-shaped sweets, chocolate rice cereals, small round chocolates
- Gifts and jewels: mini gummy sweets, foil-wrapped sweets, silver and gold hundreds and thousands
- Sheep wool: mini-marshmallows, coconut-covered mallows, candy floss
- Campfire: mini red, yellow and orange boiled or jelly sweets; red, yellow and orange liquorice strips; hard-boiled sweets (red and orange) melted on to baking parchment
- Courtyard: crushed rice-based breakfast cereals
- Paths or cobbles: sticks of chewing gum; round, mini boiled or liquorice sweets
- Tails: liquorice laces (black)
- Manger: breadsticks, chocolate bars and sticks, shaped fondant icing

Templates for clothing, faces and other details that you may wish to make from fondant icing are included with the kits for the gingerbread figures on pages 76–86.

Please note: biscuits may change shape while they are baking. Therefore, accessories made from fondant may also need to be adapted to suit.

★

Equipment and recipes

Equipment for mixing

- Food processor (optional)
- Mixing bowls
- Mixing spoons
- Measuring cups and spoons
- Saucepan
- Scales

Equipment for chilling or freezing

- Clingfilm, zip-top bags or plastic, airtight containers
- Parchment paper

Equipment for rolling, cutting and baking

- Baking paper or parchment
- Clean hard surfaces
- Cutters, knives and scissors (child-friendly if to be used by children)
- Edgeless baking sheets
- Rolling-pin

Equipment for decorating

- Bowls
- Fondant cutters
- Icing bags with decorative tips
- Spoons
- Squeezy tubes

Recipe for gingerbread dough

Ingredients

- 90g treacle or golden syrup
- 175g soft dark brown sugar
- 60g butter or margarine
- 350g plain flour
- 1 level tsp ground ginger
- 1 level tsp ground mixed spice or cinnamon
- 1 medium egg or equivalent powdered substitute
- 1 tsp baking powder (for edible figures)

This is a basic recipe for gingerbread dough. To help the cut dough maintain its shape while baking and to create pieces that are sturdy enough for construction, you will need to make it without the baking powder.

You will need a *double* batch of dough without baking powder to make the stable and one of each of the nativity figures, using the templates available for download from www.barnabasinchurches. org.uk/9780857461612/. If you are using the smaller templates provided in this book, you will be able to make more figures from the same quantity of dough.

You will need another batch of dough, with baking powder

added, to make additional pieces intended for consumption at the gingerbread family service or other gathering.

Please see 'Health, hygiene and safety' (page 14) before you start.

Method

1. Melt the treacle or golden syrup, brown sugar and butter in a large saucepan over a gentle heat, stirring until the sugar has dissolved.
2. Remove the pan from the heat and allow the mixture to cool slightly.
3. Combine the flour, baking powder, ginger and spices in a bowl.
4. Add the wet ingredients to the dry and mix together in the bowl to make a pliable dough.

To store the dough for use at a later time, see page 17; to chill and roll the dough for immediate use, see the tips on page 18.

To prepare equipment for rolling and cutting the dough, see page 18; to roll and cut the dough, see pages 18–19; to re-chill the shapes before baking, see page 19.

Transfer the cut shapes on their parchment to a baking tray and bake at 350°F/180°C/Gas 4 for 12 minutes or until the edges turn golden brown. Remove from the oven and allow to cool while still on the parchment. Store the baked shapes until ready to decorate (see page 23).

Recipe for royal icing

This icing is used for mortar, spreading, piping, flooding and painting. Royal icing is ideal for construction and decoration.

Ingredients

- 4 tsp egg white substitute
- 4 tbsp cold water
- 500g icing sugar
- Food colouring liquids or gels

Method

Combine all of the ingredients in a large mixing bowl. Beat at high speed until the icing turns very white and holds a soft peak (at least 7–10 minutes). If the mixture is too runny, whip in more sugar. Tint your icing to suit. Traditional liquid food colouring works well for lighter colours and gels for richer colours. Add the colouring a little at a time.

NB: Although royal icing can be made ahead of time, it is best used on the day that it is made, as it will separate. It also dries out easily so should be kept in an airtight container and covered when not in use.

Adapt the thickness of royal icing to your needs as follows.

- Mortar icing is the thickest icing, just soft enough to be squeezed out of a piping bag. It is best used to stick heavier shapes together (see 'Building and decorating the nativity', page 24) and to attach decorative items to shapes. To attach items, dab a spot of icing to the underside, stick it on to the shape and let it set. Mortar icing can also be spread with child-safe tools such as plastic knives or small rubber spatulas.
- Piping icing is the consistency of toothpaste. It is soft enough to squeeze out of a piping bag but thick enough to hold its shape. It is used to outline shapes (which helps to contain flooding icing), for writing and for drawing details. Special designs can also be made using decorative tips with your piping

bag. It can be spread with child-safe tools such as plastic knives or rubber spatulas.

- Flooding icing is just runny enough to flood the shape it is being poured on to. It can be applied with a spoon. However, you may find it easier (and tidier) to use a squeezy bottle with a screw-top lid.
- Painting icing is watered down to the consistency of thick paint and applied with a paintbrush. It is best to paint shapes flat and let them dry before standing them upright.

Recipe for glacé icing

This is used for spreading, piping or drizzling. Glacé icing is ideal for on-the-spot decorating and eating.

Ingredients

- 100g icing sugar
- 2 tbsp water (or orange juice, lemon juice or vanilla extract)
- Colouring of your choice

Method

1. Put the icing sugar into a bowl. Add 2 tablespoons of water or flavouring and mix to the desired thickness.
2. Add colouring (a little bit at a time) if desired.
3. Thicken by adding sugar and thin by adding water.

Recipe for fondant icing paste

This is used for rolling, cutting, draping and shaping. Fondant icing is ideal for clothing, hair, faces and other decorative shapes. If you would rather not make fondant yourself, ready-made fondant is available for purchase in a variety of colours.

Ingredients

- 1 tsp gelatine
- 5 tbsp water
- 225g icing sugar
- 1 tbsp glucose syrup
- 1 tsp glycerine

Method

1. Place gelatine in a small cup; add 1 tablespoon of water and allow the mixture to soak.

2. Put the icing sugar, 4 tablespoons of water and the glucose syrup in a pan and heat at a medium heat until the sugar dissolves, stirring constantly with a wooden spoon. Then boil the mixture for two to three minutes.

3. Heat the soaked gelatine mixture until it is dissolved into liquid (do this by putting the cup in boiling water on the hob or putting it briefly into the microwave).

4. Dip the pan of sugar mixture briefly into cold water to stop it cooking. Add the gelatine mixture and the glycerine to the sugar mixture and stir together. Pour on to a flat, greased surface.

5. Mix and fold with a large palette knife until the mixture turns into a paste.

6. Parcel the fondant icing up with clingfilm and refrigerate it overnight or until firm enough to knead easily. Remove from the fridge, unbundle and knead in the desired colour a little at a time. Liquid colouring is good for tinting; colouring paste produces stronger colours.

Use the fondant immediately or wrap tightly in several layers of clingfilm and refrigerate for up to three days.

When you are ready, roll the fondant between two sheets of baking parchment with a rolling-pin. Sprinkle the bottom sheet with icing sugar to prevent the icing from sticking.

Cut your shapes with a cutter or a child-safe knife, or simply shape with your fingers (dip your fingers in icing sugar to prevent them from sticking).

Mortar the shapes to your gingerbread with royal icing.

NB: Fondant icing of different colours can also be blended to produce new colours. Simply knead portions of two colours together.

Fake and no-bake alternatives

If, after careful consideration, you decide that a gingerbread project is too difficult for your group to undertake, you can skip the gingerbread altogether and make a fake or no-bake version. These can look effective, are easier and quicker to achieve and suit most skill levels. No-bake nativities, in particular, can be completed in a single session.

A cardboard nativity

To make a fake out of cardboard, see page 16. You can decorate your cardboard nativity scene with paint, paper, marking pens, twigs, leaves, bark, chips, buttons, ribbons, scrapbook paper, fabric and so on. You can even give your people and animals googly eyes and dust the scene with flour or sugar for a snowy effect.

A food-based, no-bake nativity

To make a no-bake nativity, use any of the items listed under 'Decorating ideas' (see page 28), as well as the additional suggestions listed below.

- Mortar and decorating: ready-made icing and ready-to-roll coloured fondant
- Stable: large ready-made square sponge cakes; sliced Battenburg or fruit cakes, cut to shape and stuck together with mortar icing; ready-made sponge rolls stuck together with mortar icing

- Roof: large rectangular rye-based savoury crackers; breadsticks
- Stars: chocolate stars
- Sheep: marshmallows for bodies; black liquorice or liquorice sweets for faces and legs
- Donkey: snack-sized chocolate bars, ready-made brown fondant icing
- Scarves and robes: fruit roll-ups, ready-made coloured fondant icing
- People: gum drops (bodies), round chocolate sweets (heads), chocolate biscuit sticks (arms and legs); shaped, ready-made marzipan or fondant icing; ready-made gingerbread people

Adapting for Messy Church

The Gingerbread Nativity is ideally suited for use in Messy Church. To achieve it successfully will require considered planning. You will need to be familiar with guidelines for health, hygiene and safety (see page 14). You will also need to read the chapter headed 'Before you start' (see page 10) and decide how it relates to your own circumstances and resources. Then, of course, you will want to let your families know (starting in October) what you are planning to do together. This will give everyone a chance to invite other families who may not yet be coming to Messy Church, make preparations if they are planning to do any baking at home, and generate a sense of anticipation befitting the Advent season ahead.

November Messy Church: a taster demo

You may wish to mix, roll, cut and bake some simple shapes (such as stars and angels) as a Messy Church activity in November. This will serve as a demonstration for families who would like to have a go at baking the pieces for their own complete scenes at home.

December Messy Church: decorating the nativity

In advance of the session, bake and assemble the gingerbread stable, or construct a cardboard stand-up background (see page 16), and bake the people and animal shapes.

Icing should be made and coloured (white, black, grey, rusty brown, yellow, pink, and so on) before the Messy Church session. Small sandwich bags with the tip of one corner cut out make great icing bags and should also be filled with icing before Messy Church. See pages 32–35 for icing recipes and 'Using icing' (page 27) for further instructions.

The decorative sweets and so on (see 'Decorating ideas' on pages 28–29) should be set out in bowls for easy identification and access.

A separate table could be set up for rolling and cutting fondant icing, with the equipment needed to do so (see pages 34–36).

During the one-hour craft session, invite all ages to decorate the people and animal shapes and create the tableau. You could also invite everyone to decorate a pre-baked star, made with baking powder, to eat or take home to remind them of Jesus' birth.

The four teaching sessions in this resource will offer ample material for families to chat about the meaning of Christmas and reflect on Christmas themes together. You may choose to use the 'Chat about...' points from one session or a combination of them all. Give each family a list of things to chat about while they decorate. You might also want to add a memory verse from one of the sessions for the family to memorise while they work. You could play some of the recommended songs or Christmas music in the background.

Use the finished nativity during the worship time. Tell a simple, clear version of the Christmas story, adding the appropriate figures to the gingerbread stable as you go along. See the 'Suggested order of service' (pages 68–70) for appropriate songs that you may wish to sing together, story references and guidance on which figures to add at which point. You may also want to include the story 'The wise men worship Jesus' (*The Barnabas Children's Bible* 250 and 251).

An alternative, more ambitious approach is to ask families to bake their own nativity pieces at home (see page 26 for a full list) and bring them to the December Messy Church to build and decorate. Volunteers from the team or from within the church or community could bake scenes for families who would rather not bake their own. Each family will need to be given a copy of the recipe and equipment needed (see pages 30–32), the instructions for mixing, rolling, cutting and baking (see pages 16–21) and a set of templates pre-cut from plastic (see pages 75–87) to take home with them. Remind them that they must also bring a board large enough for their nativity to stand on, and a container large enough to transport the decorated scene home safely. Bowls of white icing sugar will need to be supplied at the Messy Church session for mortaring the stables together and sticking things to them. You may wish to extend the Messy Church session to allow more time for the construction process. Only you will be able to decide what works best in your situation.

★ **Section 2** ★

Session plans

Each of the four sessions focuses on an Advent story and includes a reflection and suggestions for group discussion as you build and decorate your nativity scenes together. You should not aim to cover everything in the material, but use it for personal preparation. Then you can draw from it whatever will encourage a spiritually meaningful chat as you work. Younger groups may simply enjoy hearing the story in your own words or from a children's Bible and chatting about it, while older groups may enjoy a summarised version of the reflection and exploring the theme in more depth.

A Christmas song is suggested for each session. This will provide some music while tidying up and getting ready for the 'Taste of the day' blessing, which is also included for each session.

Please note that the visit of the wise men is not included in the four sessions but will provide the background and theme for the family service. Therefore, the gingerbread wise men, camels and star are to be baked but not decorated until after the family service. A giant A4 sized star (stained-glass effect or slotted if you are feeling adventurous) should be baked and decorated for use as a prop during the family service.

★

• **Session 1** •

Jesus came to keep God's promises

Reflection

When someone makes a promise, we want them to keep it. We know we can trust people who keep their promises.

It was God's plan all along to save the world through his Son, Jesus, and Jesus offered himself to save us even before people were created. However, the first time that God promised to send a Saviour (a rescuer) was just after Adam and Eve had chosen to ignore God's rule and live their own way. Nothing was as it should have been after that, and nothing could be put right again without God's help. The Saviour would be a man and Satan would be crushed by him, even though the Saviour himself would be struck down too (Genesis 3:15).

The Old Testament looks forward to the coming of the promised Saviour. His birth fulfilled prophecies that had been made as far back as 700 years before. The truths and events of Jesus' life in the New Testament are fulfilments of what God had promised through many centuries of history.

People in every generation had been watching and waiting for God to keep this promise. In fact, the Bible records hundreds of promises about when the Saviour would come, what he would be like and what he would do—even how he would die and come back to life again. Sometimes people were excited and thought that the Saviour would come soon, and sometimes it felt as if he would never come. They just set about living their lives, as we all have to do while we wait. Some forgot about God's promises, some didn't believe God's promises, and some held on to them tightly so that they wouldn't forget.

Mary loved God and wanted to serve him. She believed God's promise and was watching and waiting. She was going about her business when the angel Gabriel appeared. Mary was going to give birth to the Saviour who would keep all the promises God made— only nine more months to wait!

Session at a glance

- Read or retell the story of the angel Gabriel's visit to Mary (Luke 1:26–38) using a modern Bible translation or a children's Bible such as *The Barnabas Children's Bible* (story number 242).
- Construct the stable, the ox, the angel Gabriel and Mary.
- Chat about how we can believe God's promises.
- Listen to the song 'From heaven you came' (CMP 162) or similar.

Taste God's word: But when the time was right, God sent his Son, and a woman gave birth to him (Galatians 4:4).

Taste of the day: Jelly babies

You will need:

- Baked gingerbread shapes: Kits 1, 2, 3 and 4 (see pages 75–78 for templates)
- Reference photographs, model or videos (visit www. renitaboyle.com or www.barnabasinchurches.org.uk/ 9780857461612/)

- Equipment, items and instructions for decorating (see pages 26–29)
- A recording of 'From heaven you came' (CMP 162) or similar
- A jelly baby and Galatians 4:4 printed out for each person in the group

Storytelling

Read the story about the angel Gabriel's visit to Mary (Luke 1:26–38) using a modern Bible translation or retell the story from a children's Bible such as *The Barnabas Children's Bible*.

Gingerbread nativity construction

Begin work on the stable, the ox, the angel Gabriel and Mary (Kits 1, 2, 3 and 4 on pages 75–78). Chat together as you work.

Chat about...

- Have you been counting the days until Christmas? It can be difficult to wait, but how can we use this waiting time wisely?
- The word 'Advent' means 'coming', so perhaps we can use this time to remember how Jesus came to keep God's promises.

Chat about the story

- How did Mary feel when she saw Gabriel?
- How do you think Gabriel felt when he saw Mary?
- What was the message that God had for Mary?

- How did Mary respond to the message?
- Why did Mary sing such a joyful song (Luke 1:46–55)?
- What promises did God make to Mary and how did he keep them?
- What does it feel like when someone keeps a promise they have made?

Chat about how Jesus, the Saviour, came to keep God's promise

- The Saviour would be human and divine; both man and God (Isaiah 9:6–7; Mark 1:1; John 1:1–3, 14).
- The Saviour would be born to a virgin (Isaiah 7:14; Matthew 1:20–23).
- The Saviour would be from Galilee (Isaiah 9:1–2; Matthew 2:22–23; 4:13–16) but would be born in a small town called Bethlehem (Micah 5:2; Luke 2:6–7).
- The Saviour's ancestors would be from King David's family; in fact, King David was Jesus' ancestor (Isaiah 9:6–7; Matthew 1:6; Luke 3:31).
- The Saviour would reach out to everyone everywhere; everyone would be included in God's rescue plan (Matthew 12:14–21).
- The Saviour would heal people spiritually and physically— inside hurts and outside hurts (Isaiah 29:18; 35:5–6a; 61:1–2; Luke 4:16–21; 7:20–22).
- The Saviour would be a king but would ride on a donkey (Zechariah 9:9), and the donkey would be untamed (Matthew 21:1–7).
- The Saviour would be despised and rejected (Isaiah 53:3; Psalm 118:22; Matthew 21:42; John 7:1–5, 48–49), hated without cause (Psalm 69:4; Isaiah 49:7; John 7:48–49; 15:24–25). The crucifixion account in all the Gospels provides ample evidence of this.

- The Saviour would be betrayed for 30 pieces of silver and this silver would be returned (Zechariah 11:12–13; Matthew 26:14–15; 27:3–10).
- The Saviour would be deserted by his disciples on the very night he needed them most (Zechariah 13:7; Matthew 26:31).
- The Saviour would be crucified; he would be mocked and pierced through hands and feet but his bones would not be broken; men would gamble for his clothing (Psalm 22:7, 16–18; 34:20; Matthew 27:34–50; Mark 15:24; Luke 23:11, 33–34, 35–39; 24:36–39; John 19:17–30, 33, 36).
- The Saviour would rise from death (Psalm 16:10–11; Matthew 28:5–9; Mark 16:6; Luke 24:4–7; John 20:11–16; Acts 1:3; 2:32).

NB: Psalm 22 and Isaiah 52:13—53:12 in particular reveal events that parallel Jesus' life and death. Indeed, there are eleven prophecies in Psalm 22 alone. Isaiah told people to be strong and fearless while they waited for God to keep his promise to send the Saviour. He so accurately and beautifully portrays what would happen to Jesus that Isaiah 53 is often called 'the gospel according to Isaiah'.

Chat about how we can believe God's promises to us

- God will supply your need according to his riches in glory through Jesus Christ (Philippians 4:19).
- God's grace is sufficient for us; it is possible for us to be close to God again because of what Jesus did (2 Corinthians 12:9; Romans 5:2).
- God will help us when we are tempted (1 Corinthians 10:13).
- God has promised ultimate victory over death (Acts 2:32).
- God has promised that all things work together for good for those who love and serve him (Romans 8:28).
- God has promised salvation and forgiveness of sins (Acts 2:38).

- God has promised eternal life (John 10:27, 28).
- God has promised that all who believe in Jesus will be saved (John 3:16).

Listening

Listen to 'From heaven you came' (CMP 162) or a similar song as you tidy up.

Taste God's word

But when the time was right, God sent his Son, and a woman gave birth to him (Galatians 4:4).

Taste together

Give everyone a jelly baby and then say the Bible verse together as a blessing.

★

Session 2 •

Jesus came to be God with us

Reflection

Parents usually think long and hard about what to name their children. Names often reveal something about our family history, the circumstances of our birth or the hopes that our parents have for us. Names have meanings. This was particularly true in the Hebrew and Greek languages of Bible times. Names often described the character or purpose of the one being named.

When Mary and Joseph discovered that they were going to have a baby, they didn't think about what to name him, as most parents do. In fact, they didn't choose the baby's name at all. God did! God sent an angel to tell Mary to name the baby Jesus, which means 'God saves' (literally, 'God is salvation'). God also sent an angel to tell Joseph to name the baby Jesus because he would 'save his people from their sins'. Naming the baby Jesus would fulfil a very specific promise that God had made hundreds of years earlier: 'A virgin will have a baby boy, and he will be called "Immanuel", which means "God is with us"' (Matthew 1:23; see Isaiah 7:14).

What a wonderful truth is revealed in Jesus' naming. God did not send someone else to be our Saviour, but came himself in the person of Jesus. Jesus was fully human but also God in the flesh. He was the Word who 'became a human being and lived here with us', as John would later describe him (John 1:14). As Paul would say, 'God lives fully in Christ' (Colossians 2:9).

What an amazing message of hope! God has not abandoned us

to the problems and sorrows that happen to us or that our choices sometimes bring. God is with us, always ready to bring hope, healing, courage and strength for whatever we have to face, today and in the future. The name Jesus (God saves) describes what Jesus is able to do for us because of who he is—Immanuel, God with us. Jesus is a name that carries the hope and promise for everything that God would bring to the world. No one with sin could ever qualify to save others with sin. Perhaps this is why Peter said, 'Only Jesus has the power to save! His name is the only one in all the world that can save anyone' (Acts 4:12).

Session at a glance

- Read or retell the story about the angel Gabriel's visit to Joseph (Matthew 1:18–24) using a modern Bible translation or a children's Bible such as *The Barnabas Children's Bible* (story number 245).
- Construct Joseph and the donkey.
- Chat about how we can be like Jesus.
- Listen to the song 'Emmanuel, Emmanuel' (CMP 121) or similar.

Taste God's word: 'But I'm giving you a new commandment. You must love each other, just as I have loved you' (John 13:34–35).

Taste of the day: Jelly hearts or fresh strawberries

You will need:

- Baked gingerbread shapes: Kits 5 and 6 (see pages 79–80 for templates)

- Reference photographs, model or videos (visit www. renitaboyle.com or www.barnabasinchurches.org.uk/ 9780857461612/)
- Equipment, items and instructions for decorating (see pages 26–29)
- A recording of 'Emmanuel, Emmanuel' (CMP 121) or similar
- A jelly heart or fresh strawberry and John 13:34–35 printed out for each person in the group

Storytelling

Read the story about the angel's visit to Joseph (Matthew 1:18–24) using a modern Bible translation or retell the story from a children's Bible such as *The Barnabas Children's Bible*. Then summarise the reflection—Jesus came to be God with us—as appropriate for your group.

Gingerbread nativity construction

Begin work on Joseph and the donkey (Kits 5 and 6 on pages 79 and 80). Continue work on unfinished pieces. Begin to decorate Joseph and the donkey. Chat together as you work.

Chat about...

- Are you counting the days until Christmas? It can be difficult to wait when we're excited. How can we use this waiting time wisely?
- The word 'Advent' means 'coming'; perhaps we can use this time to remember how Jesus came to be God with us.

Chat about the story

- How did Joseph feel when he found out that Mary was going to have a baby?
- What did the angel say to Joseph?
- What did Joseph do after the angel had left?
- What was the special name that God wanted the baby to have?
- Why was this name special?

Chat about our own stories

- What special family Christmas traditions are there in your family?
- Can you tell us about a favourite gift you have given or received?
- Do you know how you got your name and what your name means? (A name book is handy here.)
- Jesus was eight days old when his family travelled to the temple for a special thanksgiving and naming ceremony. How do we celebrate the birth of babies in our culture?

Chat about how Jesus came to be God with us

- Jesus was both human and God (Isaiah 9:6–7; Mark 1:1; John 1:1–3, 14).
- How do we know that Jesus was human? (He had a physical body; he was born and died; he needed food, water and sleep; he felt human emotions and had friends.)
- How do we know that Jesus was God? (He was miraculously conceived, lived a sinless life, performed miracles and rose from the dead himself. He had insight and foreknowledge and taught with authority. Jesus claimed his own divinity and others gave evidence of it and affirmed it.)
- How does it help us to know that Jesus is both human and God with us?

Chat about how we can be like Jesus

- How did Jesus show God's love to people, and how can we do the same?
- How does the Holy Spirit help us to be like Jesus? (God's Spirit makes us loving, happy, peaceful, patient, kind, good, faithful, gentle, and self-controlled—see Galatians 5:22–23.)

Listening

Listen to the song 'Emmanuel, Emmanuel' (CMP 121) or a similar song as you tidy up.

Taste God's word

'But I'm giving you a new commandment. You must love each other, just as I have loved you' (John 13:34–35).

Taste together

Give everyone a jelly heart or a fresh strawberry and then say the Bible verse together as a blessing.

★

Jesus came to save us

Reflection

God had a plan to save us before the world began. Indeed, Jesus offered himself as the Saviour before people were created. Jesus' primary purpose was even stated by the angel Gabriel, and is in the meaning of Jesus' name: 'He will save his people from their sins' (Matthew 1:21).

That said, not everyone recognised Jesus as the Saviour when he came—at least, not as the kind of saviour they'd been hoping for. They wanted a political saviour. The Saviour would be a king, from King David's line, and kings had power. They wanted him to save them from Roman oppression. They wanted God to send a saviour-king who would bring earthly prosperity, justice and power. They wanted a king who would defeat his enemies, not be defeated by them—and certainly not by hanging bloodied, bruised and beaten on a Roman cross. They didn't reckon on the resurrection!

People, then and now, want to be saved from many things, including failure, poverty, ill-health, broken relationships, shame and death. It is good to know that God's plan to save us includes the fallout from our sin—those situations we find ourselves in as well as those we cause through the choices we make independently from God. However, Jesus came to save us from even more than this. The primary purpose of Jesus' life was not to deliver us from the consequences of sin but to deliver us from the power of sin to separate us from our Creator and all that we were created to be.

Jesus' death and resurrection did what was impossible for any other person to do and delivered on the promise to meet our deepest need. We will one day be free from the presence of sin altogether. We will be in the company of God.

Session at a glance

- Read or retell the story about Jesus being born (Luke 2:1–7), using a modern Bible translation or a children's Bible such as *The Barnabas Children's Bible* (story numbers 246 and 247).
- Construct the baby Jesus, the big star and little stars (optional).
- Chat about how we can be close to God.
- Listen to the song 'See him lying in a bed of straw' (CMP 589) or similar.

Taste God's word: God loved the people of this world so much that he gave his only Son, so that everyone who has faith in him will have eternal life and never really die (John 3:16).

Taste of the day: Chocolate biscuit cross (two finger-shaped chocolate biscuits formed into a cross with a dab of royal icing)

You will need:

- Baked gingerbread shapes: Kits 7 and 8 (see pages 81–82 for templates)
- Reference photographs, model or videos (visit www.renitaboyle.com or www.barnabasinchurches.org.uk/9780857461612/)
- Equipment, items and instructions for decorating (see pages 26–29)

- A recording of 'See him lying in a bed of straw' (CMP 589) or similar
- A chocolate biscuit cross and John 3:16 printed out for each person in the group

Storytelling

Read the story about Jesus' birth (Luke 2:1–7) using a modern Bible translation or retell the story from a children's Bible such as *The Barnabas Children's Bible*. Then summarise the reflection—Jesus came to save us—as appropriate for your group.

Gingerbread nativity construction

Begin to decorate baby Jesus, the large star and small stars (Kits 7 and 8 on pages 81–82). Continue work on unfinished pieces. Chat together as you work.

Chat about...

- Are you counting the days until Christmas? It can be difficult to wait when we're excited. How can we use this waiting time wisely?
- The word 'Advent' means 'coming'; perhaps we can use this time to remember how Jesus came to save us.

Chat about the story

- What is a census and why are people counted?
- How does it feel to be in a busy place with lots of people?

- How do you think it felt for Mary and Joseph to travel?
- What do you think the stable was like?
- How did Mary and Joseph feel when Jesus was born?
- What are babies like just after they are born?

Chat about why Jesus came

- How would you describe what the word 'sin' means?
- How does living our own way affect our relationship with God, others, ourselves and our world?
- Why can't we put things right without Jesus' help?

Chat about how we can be close to God

- Why did Jesus die on the cross?
- Why does Jesus' resurrection give us hope?
- How can we decide to live God's way?
- What kinds of things can we do to help us to live God's way (pray, read our Bible, meet with others, talk to others about Jesus)?
- How can we follow Jesus' example in the way we live our lives (how he treated people, what he chose to do with his time, the attitude he had)?

Listening

Listen to the song 'See him lying in a bed of straw' (CMP 589) or a similar song as you tidy up.

Taste God's word

God loved the people of this world so much that he gave his only Son, so that everyone who has faith in him will have eternal life and never really die (John 3:16).

Taste together

Give everyone two chocolate finger-shaped biscuits. Shape into a cross with a dab of royal icing and then say the Bible verse together as a blessing.

★

Jesus came to bring good news

Reflection

Have you ever written a mission statement—a plan for what you want to accomplish and how you will accomplish it? At the beginning of Jesus' ministry, he read out his own mission statement from Isaiah 61:1–2 (see Luke 4:16–22). It was a specific promise from the Old Testament about what the Saviour would do when he came. Jesus wanted people to know what kind of good news he would be bringing. He also wanted people to know that he would be fulfilling the promises of God in doing so.

He read, 'The Lord's Spirit has come to me, because he has chosen me to tell the good news to the poor. The Lord has sent me to announce freedom for prisoners, to give sight to the blind, to free everyone who suffers, and to say, "This is the year the Lord has chosen"' (Luke 4:18–19).

The good news is that no matter what may trouble or restrict us, Jesus can set us free. We can be free from sin's power when we rest in and rely on Jesus.

He came to bring good news to the poor—to help those who are broken-hearted, shattered, trampled, crushed and bruised. He came to embrace us and to heal those areas of our lives where we hurt. As we are comforted, we can bring comfort.

He came to free those who are captive—unable to live freely because of the wrong done to them or the wrong they do. In Christ we can break free from the regrets and sorrows of the past and look hopefully to the future.

He came to liberate those who are imprisoned—those who are oppressed by poverty, depression and despair. He gave us liberty: in Christ we can forgive and be forgiven. Jesus preached the message of forgiveness from God and forgiveness toward others. Knowing and accepting our need for God's forgiveness gives us a new perspective about our need to forgive others. True freedom can only come from this release (Matthew 18:21–35).

Session at a glance

- Read or retell the story about the shepherds visiting Jesus (Luke 2:8–20) using a modern Bible translation or a children's Bible such as *The Barnabas Children's Bible* (story number 248).
- Construct angels (optional), shepherds and sheep.
- Chat about how we can bring good news to others.
- Listen to the song 'Hark! the herald angels sing' or similar.

Taste God's word: 'Don't be afraid! I have good news for you, which will make everyone happy' (Luke 2:10).

Taste of the day: Liquorice allsorts

You will need:

- Baked gingerbread shapes: Kits 3 (optional), 9 and 10 (see pages 77 and 83–84 for templates)
- Reference photographs, model or videos (visit www. renitaboyle.com or www.barnabasinchurches.org.uk/ 9780857461612/)
- Equipment, items and instructions for decorating (see pages 26–29)

- A recording of 'Hark! the herald angels sing' (MP3 211) or similar
- A liquorice allsort and Luke 2:10 printed out for each person in the group

Storytelling

Read the story about the shepherds visiting Jesus (Luke 2:8–20) using a modern Bible translation or retell the story from a children's Bible such as *The Barnabas Children's Bible*. Then summarise the reflection—Jesus came to bring good news—as appropriate for your group.

Gingerbread nativity construction

Begin work on the angels, shepherds and sheep (see Kits 3, 9 and 10 on pages 77 and 83–84). Continue work on unfinished pieces. Begin to decorate the shepherds, sheep and angels. Chat together as you work.

Chat about...

- Are you counting the days until Christmas? It can be difficult to wait when we're excited. How can we use this waiting time wisely?
- The word 'Advent' means 'coming'; perhaps we can use this time to remember how Jesus came to bring good news.

Chat about the story

- How do shepherds look after their sheep at night?
- What do you think the shepherds heard before the angels arrived?
- Why do you think the shepherds were afraid of the angels?
- Why didn't the angels want the shepherds to be afraid?
- What do you think angels sound like when they sing?
- What do you think the good news was, and why was it such good news?
- Why do you think the shepherds ran to see Jesus?
- How do you think the shepherds felt when they saw Jesus?
- Who do you think the shepherds told afterwards, and what do you think they might have said?
- What do you think Mary was thinking about as Jesus slept that night?

Chat about good news

- Can you remember a time when bad news was replaced with good news in your life?
- How does it feel to get good news?
- Why is Jesus such good news?

Chat about how we can share the good news of Jesus with others

- What is your favourite story about Jesus?
- Can you think of one friend that you would like to tell about Jesus?
- How can you tell others about Jesus with your actions?

Listening

Listen to the song 'Hark! the herald angels sing' (MP3 211) or a similar song as you tidy up.

Taste God's word

'Don't be afraid! I have good news for you, which will make everyone happy' (Luke 2:10).

Taste together

Give everyone a liquorice sweet and then say the Bible verse together as a blessing.

Jesus came to be God's gift

The family service is an opportunity for your group to display their gingerbread nativities and share the joy of the Christmas story with the church, community and other invited family and friends.

You will need:

- Baked or cardboard gingerbread shapes to decorate the gathering space or the tree
- A display of the gingerbread nativity scenes that your group has made
- An additional nativity scene that also includes a camel (Kit 11) and wise men (Kit 12), to be used during the service
- A giant edible gingerbread star or specially decorated star to be used as an object lesson (Kit 13)
- Stories and hymns as outlined below
- Baked gingerbread shapes simply decorated with glacé icing to eat: particularly angels (Kit 3), stars (Kit 8) and sheep (Kit 10)
- 'Taste of the day' snacks and verses (see below)

Before the service:

- Think creatively about how you will decorate your church or other gathering space.
- Display the nativity scenes your group has made on a specially decorated table or several smaller tables around the space.
- Hang simple undecorated gingerbread shapes on the Christmas tree, on pew ends or on the backs of chairs, or include them in floral arrangements. Angels, sheep and stars are particularly appropriate as there are so many of these in the Christmas story. NB: You will need to announce that hanging decorations are for display purposes only.
- If the thought of making enough gingerbread shapes to decorate your tree or space is too daunting, make paper or card versions instead. You may wish to involve a different group altogether in decorating the church.

Gingerbread nativity preparation

During the first part of the service, each of the four Advent stories previously explored by your group may be retold. Songs that your group have listened to while making their nativities may be sung. Appropriate gingerbread pieces can be added to a gingerbread stable between the story and the song. Remember to make a camel and wise man, which can be added during the closing song at the end of the service.

You may want to make an additional nativity scene specifically for this purpose or choose one from among those made by your group. If you choose to make an additional scene, it may be given as a gift to someone in your congregation or a community group after the service is over.

The empty gingerbread stable (on its board) should be placed in a prominent position in front of the church (or other space) before the service begins. It will need to be easily accessible, with plenty of room to add nativity pieces to it as the service progresses.

A few days before the service, choose children or other members of the congregation to read each story, so that they have time to practise. Also choose those who will place the nativity pieces in the stable and make sure they know when to do so (see service running order below).

Family-friendly talk

A family-friendly talk will form the second part of the service. The focus of this talk will be on the kingship of the Messiah (Isaiah 9: 6–7) and the visit of the wise men (Matthew 2:1–21). The content of the talk should be decided by your minister/speaker. However, a suggested theme might be how Jesus came to be God's gift.

You may want to bake and decorate an A4 (or larger) Christmas star for the speaker to use as a visual aid. This can simply be a giant gingerbread biscuit or (for greater effect) one created with a stained-glass effect (see page 21). If the gingerbread is fresh, the minister/speaker could offer people an opportunity to break a piece off and eat it at an appropriate time during the talk, or everyone could enjoy nibbling on it after the service is over.

Chocolate coins and the accompanying verse, 'God has also said that he gave us eternal life and this life comes to us from his Son' (1 John 5:11), could be handed out to the congregation and used in the blessing. Everyone could say the verse together before eating the coins.

Fellowship time

Lay on a gingerbread-themed fellowship/coffee time after the service. Include the 'Taste of the day' snacks and verses (used with the children during the making of their nativities) among the gingerbread angels and stars on offer (see below).

Also offer an opportunity for the congregation to decorate a few gingerbread biscuits of their own—particularly wise men, camels and stars. Set up a table and provide plastic knives, paper napkins, plates of undecorated gingerbread shapes, bowls of glacé icing (see page 34) and hundreds and thousands or similar decorations.

Remember to send the nativity scenes home with those who made them.

'Taste of the day' snacks and verses

- Jelly babies: 'But when the time was right, God sent his Son, and a woman gave birth to him' (Galatians 4:4).
- Jelly hearts or strawberries: 'But I'm giving you a new commandment. You must love each other, just as I have loved you' (John 13:34–35).
- Chocolate biscuit cross: God loved the people of this world so much that he gave his only Son, so that everyone who has faith in him will have eternal life and never really die (John 3:16).
- Liquorice allsorts: 'Don't be afraid! I have good news for you, which will make everyone happy' (Luke 2:10).
- Chocolate coins: 'God has also said that he gave us eternal life and this life comes to us from his Son' (1 John 5:11).

Suggested order of service

Welcome

Welcome everyone to the service. Briefly describe the gingerbread nativity project undertaken by your group. Draw attention to the scenes on display and the gingerbread decorations on the tree and elsewhere. Explain that you will be using one of the scenes and *The Barnabas Children's Bible* to tell the story of the first Christmas.

Opening prayer

Opening hymn

Old Testament reading

This reading is about the kingship of the Messiah and was written 700 years before Jesus was born.

A child has been born for us. We have been given a son who will be our ruler. His names will be Wonderful Adviser and Mighty God, Eternal Father and Prince of Peace. His power will never end; peace will last for ever. He will rule David's kingdom and make it grow strong. He will always rule with honesty and justice. The Lord All-Powerful will make certain that all of this is done.
ISAIAH 9:6–7

Gingerbread nativity

- Story 1: The angel Gabriel visits Mary (Luke 1:26–38; *Barnabas Children's Bible* 242)
- Stable scene: Add ox, Mary and angel Gabriel
- Song: 'From heaven you came' (CMP 162) or other

- Story 2: An angel visits Joseph (Matthew 1:18–24; *Barnabas Children's Bible* 245)
- Stable scene: Add Joseph and the donkey
- Song: 'Emmanuel, Emmanuel' (CMP 121) or other

- Story 3: Jesus is born (Luke 2:1–7; *Barnabas Children's Bible* 246 and 247)
- Stable scene: Add baby Jesus
- Song: 'See him lying on a bed of straw' (CMP 589) or other

- Story 4: The shepherds visit Jesus (Luke 2:8–20; *Barnabas Children's Bible* 248)
- Stable scene: Add angels (optional), shepherds and sheep
- Song: 'Hark! the herald angels sing' (MP3 211) or other

Family talk

Theme of the service: Jesus came to be God's gift. Read from the New Testament: the wise men worship Jesus (Matthew 2:1–21; *Barnabas Children's Bible* 250 and 251). Use a giant gingerbread star as a visual aid. Add king and camel to the stable.

Closing prayer

Song

'Come and join the celebration' (CMP 83)

Blessing

★ Appendix ★

★

Patterns and templates

The templates in this resource have been presented to help you easily identify which gingerbread pieces and patterns for clothing and other features you will need to include in each kit.

For the purpose of cutting your gingerbread figures from dough, however, it may be useful to know that all of the stands are the same size and that the same basic body figure No. 1 is used for Mary, Joseph and the shepherd. You will therefore need to make only one stand template (see ox stand) and one basic body (see Mary) from acetate in order to cut your dough.

Here is a ticklist of the acetate templates you will need for cutting dough.

- 1 side
- 1 back/roof
- 1 stand (see ox)
- 1 ox
- 1 angel A
- 1 angel B
- 1 angel C
- 1 basic body No. 1 (see Mary)
- 1 donkey A
- 1 donkey B back/front
- 1 donkey B head
- 1 oval
- 1 manger side
- 1 manger end
- 1 manger bottom
- 1 star A
- 1 star B centre star

- 1 star C slotted shape
- 1 star C stand
- 1 sheep
- 1 camel
- 1 basic body No. 2 (see king)

Here is a ticklist of all the pieces you will need to cut and bake for a complete nativity. Please note: you may want to make and bake extra pieces in case of accidents.

- 2 sides
- 1 wall
- 1 roof
- 1 ox
- 1 angel (A, B or C)
- 3 basic bodies No. 1 (Mary, Joseph, shepherd)
- 1 donkey A or
- 2 donkey back/front and 1 donkey head to create donkey B
- 1 oval (baby Jesus)
- 2 manger sides
- 2 manger ends
- 1 manger bottom
- 1 star (A or B) or
- 1 slotted star and 1 star stand to create star C
- 1 sheep
- 1 camel
- 1–3 basic bodies No. 2 (kings)
- 10–13 stands

For the purpose of cutting clothing and other features from rolled fondant, it may be useful to know that all the adult faces are the same shape, as are all the tunics, all the robes and all the veils. You will therefore need to cut only one acetate template for each of these shapes per nativity project.

Here is a ticklist of fondant patterns you may like to cut from acetate.

- 1 adult face (see Mary)
- 1 baby face (see Jesus)
- 1 oval (Jesus' blanket)
- 1 half oval (Jesus' blanket)
- 1 tunic (see Mary)
- 1 veil back (see Mary)
- 1 veil front (see Mary)
- 1 robe (see Joseph)
- 1 donkey blanket (see donkey A)
- 1 camel blanket (see camel)
- 1 crown (see king)

KIT 1: LEAN-TO STABLE

(2 sides, 1 back, 1 roof from gingerbread)

Stable may be constructed as follows:

(A) (B) or (C)

(A) With roof slanting forward and large gap between back and roof

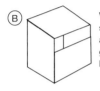

(B) With roof slanting back and small gap between back and roof

(C) With no back wall at all

2 sides from gingerbread

Cut here for stable back/roof

STABLE BACK AND STABLE ROOF
1 for the roof from gingerbread
1 for the back from gingerbread

KIT 2: OX

(1 ox and 2 stands from gingerbread)

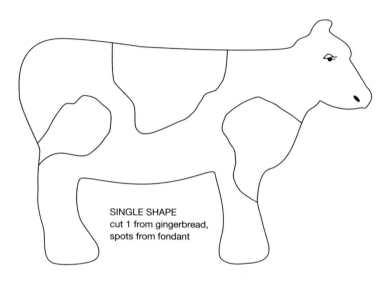

SINGLE SHAPE
cut 1 from gingerbread,
spots from fondant

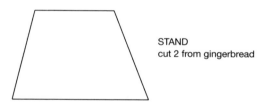

STAND
cut 2 from gingerbread

KIT 3: ANGELS

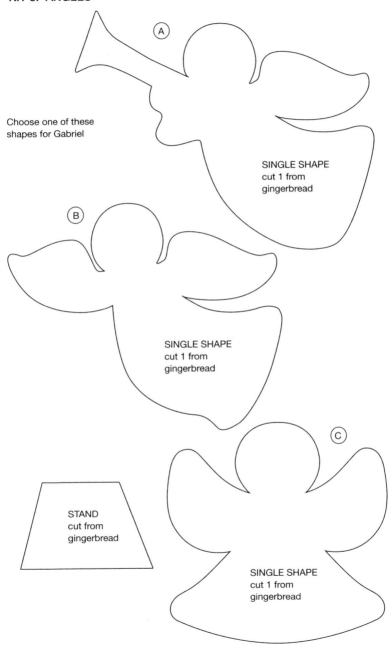

(A)

Choose one of these shapes for Gabriel

SINGLE SHAPE
cut 1 from
gingerbread

(B)

SINGLE SHAPE
cut 1 from
gingerbread

(C)

STAND
cut from
gingerbread

SINGLE SHAPE
cut 1 from
gingerbread

KIT 4: MARY

BASIC BODY 1
cut 1 from
gingerbread

VEIL BACK
cut 1 from
fondant

VEIL HEADDRESS
cut 1 from fondant

FACE
cut 1 from
fondant

STAND
cut 1 from
gingerbread

TUNIC
cut 1 from
fondant

Please note that fondant may need to be cut or stretched to fit

KIT 5: JOSEPH

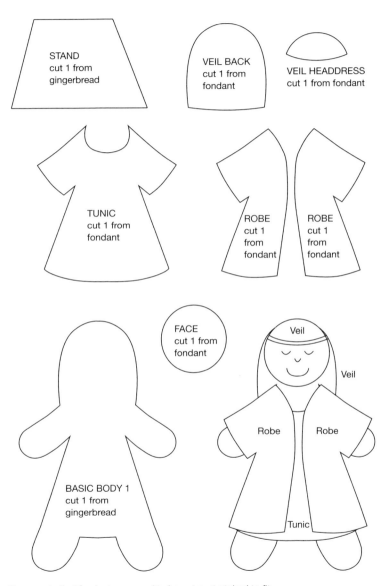

STAND
cut 1 from
gingerbread

VEIL BACK
cut 1 from
fondant

VEIL HEADDRESS
cut 1 from fondant

TUNIC
cut 1 from
fondant

ROBE
cut 1
from
fondant

ROBE
cut 1
from
fondant

FACE
cut 1 from
fondant

BASIC BODY 1
cut 1 from
gingerbread

Veil

Veil

Robe

Robe

Tunic

Please note that fondant may need to be cut or stretched to fit

KIT 6: DONKEY

(A) or (B)

BLANKET
cut 1 from
fondant

(A)

**SINGLE
SHAPE**
cut 1 from
gingerbread

STAND
cut 2 from
gingerbread and
attach behind to legs

Size of Ginger
Cream or other
purchased
biscuit

(B)

HEAD
cut 1 from
gingerbread

Cut and bake the
pieces for the
donkey.
Stick the head to
the front side with
icing and sandwich
front to back with 3
biscuits in between.
Donkey will stand.

**BACK SIDE and
FRONT SIDE**
cut 2 from
gingerbread

Circular
biscuits

Head

Back

Front

 Reproduced with permission from *The Gingerbread Nativity* by Renita Boyle (Barnabas for Children, 2013)

KIT 7: BABY JESUS AND MANGER

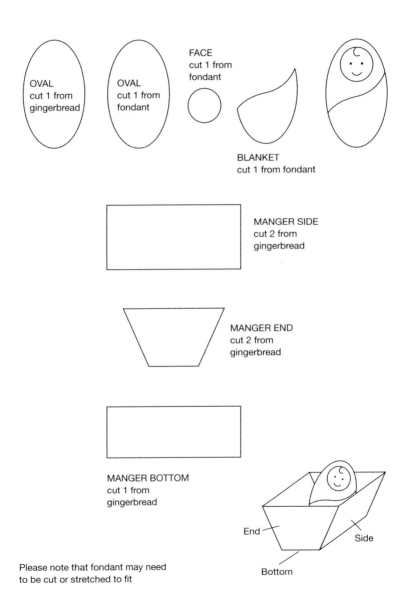

OVAL
cut 1 from
gingerbread

OVAL
cut 1 from
fondant

FACE
cut 1 from
fondant

BLANKET
cut 1 from fondant

MANGER SIDE
cut 2 from
gingerbread

MANGER END
cut 2 from
gingerbread

MANGER BOTTOM
cut 1 from
gingerbread

End

Side

Bottom

Please note that fondant may need
to be cut or stretched to fit

KIT 8: STARS

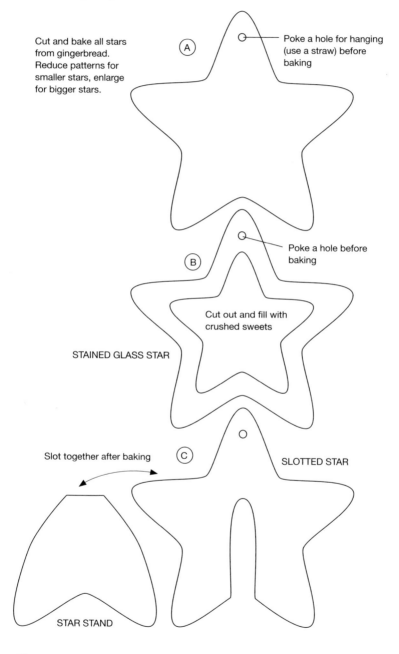

Cut and bake all stars from gingerbread. Reduce patterns for smaller stars, enlarge for bigger stars.

A

Poke a hole for hanging (use a straw) before baking

B

Poke a hole before baking

Cut out and fill with crushed sweets

STAINED GLASS STAR

Slot together after baking

C

SLOTTED STAR

STAR STAND

KIT 9: SHEPHERD

VEIL BACK
cut 1 from
fondant

VEIL
HEADDRESS
cut 1 from
fondant

TUNIC
cut 1 from
fondant

STAND
cut 1 from
gingerbread

FACE
cut 1 from
fondant

BASIC BODY 1
cut 1 from
gingerbread

Please note that fondant may need to be cut or stretched to fit

KIT 10: SHEEP

(1 sheep, 1 stand)

SINGLE SHAPE
cut 1 from
gingerbread

STAND
cut 1 from
gingerbread

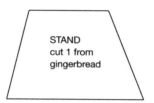

KIT 11: CAMEL

STAND
cut 1 from
gingerbread

BLANKET
cut 1 from fondant

BODY
cut 1 from gingerbread

KIT 12: WISE MEN

CROWN
cut 1 from
fondant

TUNIC
cut 1 from
fondant

ROBE
cut 1
from
fondant

ROBE
cut 1
from
fondant

STAND
cut 1 from
gingerbread

BASIC BODY 2
cut 1 from
gingerbread

Please note that fondant may need to
be cut or stretched to fit

KIT 13: LARGE STAR

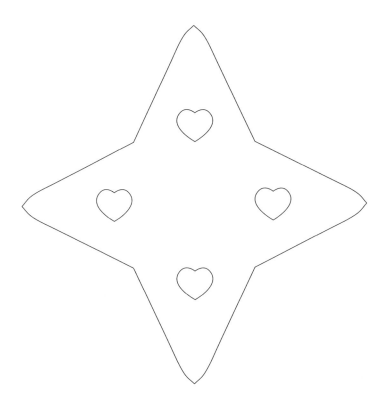

Cut required shapes (hearts, stars etc.) into the dough and fill with crushed sweets before baking or roll hundreds and thousands or edible glitter into the dough before baking. This will make a very special large star for your congregation to enjoy together at the family service.

About the author

Renita Boyle has been described as 'a remarkable storyteller—a powerball of imagination and inventiveness, who can keep young audiences spellbound and older listeners thinking'. She is listed among the professional storytellers in the *Scottish Storytelling Directory*. She is an experienced children's worker and has a BA (Hons) in Theology. She has written many books for BRF's Barnabas for Children imprint, including *Parachute Fun for Everyone* and *My Storytime Bible* (both published in 2011). Renita is married to Eric, the minister of Kirkcowan and Wigtown parish churches. They have one son, Jude, and live in Wigtown, Scotland's national book town, which is famed for its annual book festival. You can contact Renita at http://renitaboyle.com.

Seasonal Activities for Christmas Festivities

Three five-week programmes exploring the true meaning of Christmas with 7–11s

Vicki Howie

Seasonal Activities for Christmas Festivities provides three exciting programme ideas. Each programme contains five sessions that fit readily into the autumn half-term leading up to Christmas, and includes an optional short presentation for a Christmas service or related event.

Choose from three stand-alone but interrelated themes, each unpacked through icebreakers, discussions, games, crafts, dramatised Bible stories, prayers and take-home activities.

- Christmas unwrapped: Explore the parts played by five nativity characters in the Christmas story and discover how we can reflect their gifts and attitudes today.
- Christmas unpacked: Link five key Bible stories from creation to Easter to tell the great story of God's love for us and to discover why we celebrate Christmas.
- The gift of Christmas: Find out how five nativity characters symbolised the people Jesus came to befriend and think about those God wants us to remember at Christmas time.

ISBN 978 1 84101 853 9   £8.99
Available from your local Christian bookshop or, in case of difficulty, direct from BRF: please visit www.brfonline.org.uk

Family Fun for Christmas

30 Advent and Christmas activities
for families to share

Jane Butcher

Family Fun for Christmas will help you to share the meaning of Advent and Christmas with your children in 30 'family moments', to explore faith in the home and to have lots of fun together in the process. The activities are structured to take the family through the season of Advent to Christmas Day and on into the New Year.

ISBN 978 0 85746 063 9   £4.99

Available from your local Christian bookshop or, in case of difficulty, direct from BRF: please visit www.brfonline.org.uk

Messy Christmas

3 complete sessions and a treasure trove of craft ideas for Advent, Christmas and Epiphany

Lucy Moore and Jane Leadbetter

Three complete sessions for Advent, Christmas and Epiphany, together with a wealth of creative activities and crafts to extend the range of excitingly messy activities for your Messy Church. Sections include creative Christmas prayers, global action suggestions, games and competitions, Christmas food crafts and many other ideas to take you on into the New Year.

ISBN 978 0 85746 091 2   £5.99
Available from your local Christian bookshop or, in case of difficulty, direct from BRF: please visit www.brfonline.org.uk

Messy Nativity

How to run your very own Messy Nativity Advent project

Jane Leadbetter

Find out about a new project uniting communities around the nativity story at Christmas time!

* Hunt for knitted sheep in shops around town.
* Go house to house with the Christmas story.
* Perform a Messy street nativity play.

This book describes how Messy Nativity started in Liverpool in 2010, and gives a step-by-step guide to how other churches can embark on their own local Messy Nativity Advent project.

ISBN 978 0 85746 055 4   £4.99
Available from your local Christian bookshop or, in case of difficulty, direct from BRF: please visit www.brfonline.org.uk

Ten-Minute Christmas Activity Book

Bethan James and Heather Stuart

Find out what happened at the first Christmas!

The story of the birth of Jesus is combined with on-the-page puzzles and activities, perfect as a Christmas holiday book. But the story doesn't end there! Read about the events that followed the first Christmas Day.

This busy activity book will provide hours of creativity in the countdown to Christmas.

ISBN 978 0 85746 137 7   £3.99
Available from your local Christian bookshop or, in case of difficulty, direct from BRF: please visit www.brfonline.org.uk

Enjoyed

this book?

Write a review—we'd love to hear what you think.
Email: reviews@brf.org.uk

Keep up to date—receive details of our new books as they happen.
Sign up for email news and select your interest groups at:
www.brfonline.org.uk/findoutmore/

Follow us on Twitter @brfonline

By post—to receive new title information by post (UK only), complete the form below and post to: BRF Mailing Lists, 15 The Chambers, Vineyard, Abingdon, Oxfordshire, OX14 3FE

Your Details
Name _____
Address_____
_____
Town/City _____ Post Code _____
Email _____

Your Interest Groups (*Please tick as appropriate)

☐ Advent/Lent	☐ Messy Church
☐ Bible Reading & Study	☐ Pastoral
☐ Children's Books	☐ Prayer & Spirituality
☐ Discipleship	☐ Resources for Children's Church
☐ Leadership	☐ Resources for Schools

Support your local bookshop
Ask about their new title information schemes.